Shadow Appliqué

A Fresh Take
on a
Traditional
Technique

Hetty
van Boven

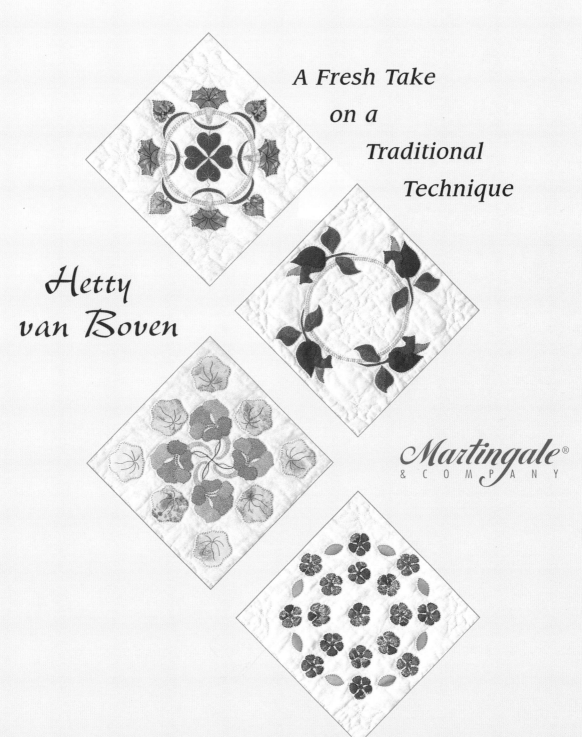

Martingale®
& COMPANY

DEDICATION

To Gerry, who never doubts my abilities,
even when I think I know better!

CREDITS

President ✍ Nancy J. Martin
CEO ✍ Daniel J. Martin
Publisher ✍ Jane Hamada
Editorial Director ✍ Mary V. Green
Managing Editor ✍ Tina Cook
Technical Editor ✍ Janet Wickell
Copy Editor ✍ Ellen Balstad
Design Director ✍ Stan Green
Illustrator ✍ Laurel Strand
Cover and Text Designer ✍ Regina Girard
Photographer ✍ Brent Kane

That Patchwork Place® is an imprint
of Martingale & Company®.

Shadow Appliqué:
A Fresh Take on a Traditional Technique
© 2003 by Hetty van Boven

Martingale & Company
20205 144th Avenue NE
Woodinville, WA 98072-8478 USA
www.martingale-pub.com

Printed in China
08 07 06 05 04 03   8 7 6 5 4 3 2 1

The information in this book is presented in good faith, but no warranty is given nor results guaranteed. Since Martingale & Company has no control over choice of materials or procedures, the company assumes no responsibility for the use of this information.

MISSION STATEMENT

Dedicated to providing quality products
and service to inspire creativity.

Library of Congress Cataloging-in-Publication Data

Boven, Hetty van.
    Shadow appliqué: a fresh take on a traditional technique / Hetty van Boven.
        p. cm.
    ISBN 1-56477-507-0
    1. Appliqué. 2. Quilting. I. Title.
    TT779 .B68 2003
    746 . 46—dc21
                                    2003009367

Contents

Introduction

Shadow appliqué is a simple appliqué technique that gets its name from the subtle shadow created when a piece of organza is positioned over an appliqué block. Fusible web, a thin material that becomes an adhesive when heated and pressed, is used to attach appliqué pieces to a background. The organza, which is placed over the work, gives it a soft, elegant look. To complete the technique, the appliqué edges are secured by hand with embroidery floss. For pillow covers, wall hangings, or quilts, you can add batting and backing and quilt the project by hand or machine.

In 1985, Yvonne Amico's book *Shadow Appliqué* introduced me to this lovely technique. After reading the book, I made some pillows and soon began to teach shadow appliqué myself. It has been on my list of workshops ever since. I have taught shadow appliqué in Australia, Canada, the Netherlands, the United States, and on Norfolk Island. Students everywhere love it because they do not have to turn under seams or spend time tracing a design onto a background. And with this method, working with sharp points and deep curves is as easy as appliquéing straight lines.

Now that you're familiar with my enthusiasm for this method, you'll understand that it was with great excitement that I designed the blocks and projects for this book. They are filled with sensuously curving flowers that even beginners can handle, and they are enhanced with a sprinkling of glamorous fabrics. I know it's the easiest method of hand appliqué you'll ever do.

The book begins with general instructions for shadow appliqué. I explain the materials and methods used and give step-by-step instructions on how to make a shadow appliqué block. Twelve exquisite floral blocks, a charming pillow cover, and a gorgeous wall hanging follow.

Make sure to read all of the instructions before you begin. Understanding the basic techniques will make the construction process enjoyable and satisfying.

Keep stitching!

Hetty

The following section describes the materials you will use to construct your shadow appliqué project. These materials include basic tools and supplies; the three types of fabric you will need—background, appliqué, and organza; fusible web; and embroidery floss.

Basic Tools and Supplies

The following are basic tools and supplies that you will need for shadow appliqué:

- A packet of assorted crewel or embroidery needles
- Straight pins, safety pins, thimble, and scissors
- A light-colored pencil if using a dark background
- A fine (0.5 mm) permanent marker
- Cream or white thread for basting
- A quilter's cutting mat, ruler, and rotary cutter
- Parchment paper or appliqué pressing mat
- A mechanical pencil with 2B lead
- An iron
- An ironing board or pad
- Sizes 11 and 12 sewing-machine needles
- Sewing machine

Background Fabrics

To create a classic look, choose light-colored background fabrics in solid-color or cream tone-on-tone cottons. A light-colored background also offers a bonus: it makes it easy for you to see the design diagram when it is positioned underneath the fabric and used as a placement guide for appliqué pieces.

Appliqué Fabrics

Any fabrics that can be used with fusible web, including metallics and satins, are suitable for shadow appliqué. Solid-colored fabrics work, but you'll find that prints add more visual texture, highlights, and shadows to things like flowers and leaves. Hand-dyed and marbled fabrics are especially effective in shadow appliqué. Within an individual piece, do not use prints that have high contrast areas unless you are certain that is what you are looking for. The areas of high contrast will compete with a petal's shape and the flower's definition will be lost.

Suitable Fabrics for Shadow Appliqué *Unsuitable Fabrics for Shadow Appliqué*

When choosing fabrics, also consider how the quilt will be used. Satin and metallic fabrics are great for a wall hanging but they are not suitable for a baby quilt that will be washed frequently.

Using a single color in a variety of shades creates more interest than using the same shade for all the appliqué pieces in a block. For example, if a design has two types of leaves, use a different green fabric for each type. If a design has both flowers and flower buds, use a different shade of purple for each shape. If a flower has a number of petals, cut petal pieces from several shades of the same color or from different prints of the same shade.

*Different prints in the same shade
add interest and depth to a flower.*

If you want a particular part of a print to appear on an appliqué piece, such as a printed flower that's centered within a circular design, use fussy cutting. When you fussy cut, you control the position of parts of a fabric print on an appliqué piece. Fussy cutting usually increases the yardage requirements, since the number of pieces you can cut depends on how the design is printed on the fabric.

Suitable Fabrics for Fussy Cutting

Fussy Cutting of Iris

Organza Overlay

I used fine, polyester organza as an overlay in all the floral blocks for this book. Cream organza on a cream background produces a classic look. Try navy, black, or burgundy organza for a dramatic effect.

Organza is much easier to tear than to cut. It frays easily, so always tear pieces that are at least 2" larger than the finished size of the blocks they will cover. The excess will be trimmed away before you assemble your project. Look for organza in the bridal department of fabric shops and be sure to note the pressing instructions before you leave the store.

Hetty's Hint

To preshrink cottons and check for colorfastness, soak each fabric separately in hot water. Let the water cool; then remove the fabrics and allow them to line dry. This method leaves that crisp, new feel of the fabrics intact. Note that I don't preshrink metallic fabrics or organza.

Fusible Web

Fusible web is a wonderful product that provides much more versatility than you can achieve using traditional appliqué methods. Fusible web is sheer and becomes adhesive when pressed with heat, enabling two fabrics to be fused together. When you buy fusible web, one side is backed with paper and the other side is ready to be fused to fabric. The paper side feels smooth and the adhesive side feels rough. Purchase the lightest-weight fusible web available. Avoid the type that is marked "no-sew" because it will be too thick to sew through.

When using fusible web for appliqué, there is no need to make pattern templates. You can trace the appliqué patterns directly onto the paper side of the fusible web, which is what I instruct in this book. Note that tracing a pattern onto fusible web reverses the pattern. For instance, if you trace a bird that faces to the left, it will face right in your finished piece of appliqué. In this book, I have reversed all appliqué patterns for you so that your finished blocks will look like the ones shown in the photos.

The following tips will help you get the best results from fusible web:

- Do not buy fusible web if the paper and adhesive layers are beginning to separate.

- Do not fold fusible web; instead, roll it on a cardboard tube.

- Use a permanent marker when tracing patterns onto the paper backing. A marker makes a darker line than a pencil and eliminates the problem of graphite transferring to the iron, and from the iron onto your fabrics.

- Press your fabrics smooth before fusing, since any folds and creases will become permanent.

- Use a dry iron to fuse the fusible web to the wrong side of the appliqué fabric.

- Do not worry about grain lines. Once fabrics are fused, they will no longer stretch.

- Use a steam setting on your iron to fuse the cut appliqué pieces to the background.

- Different brands of fusible web require different temperatures for fusing. Some brands will fuse correctly when the iron is set at "wool" but not at "cotton." For others, it is the other way around. Read the instructions and experiment on scraps of fabric.

- Applying pressure as you iron will help the fusing process.

- Keep your iron clean! I prefer to use an iron with a nonstick sole plate for all fusible work. If adhesive accidentally gets onto a nonstick surface, it is easy to wipe off with a clean cloth. Adhesive that is allowed to remain on the iron will turn into a black, burned mess that can transfer unexpectedly to a pristine block and spoil it.

- Use an appliqué mat or parchment paper between the iron and the fusible web to protect both the iron and the ironing board.

Embroidery Floss

Use embroidery floss to secure the appliqué pieces. The floss color you choose makes a big difference in the overall appearance of the project. For a soft, muted look, choose a color that blends with the appliqué fabric after it has been covered with organza. For a bolder look, choose a darker or brighter shade of floss.

Only three simple stitches are sewn with embroidery floss in the projects: a running stitch, stem stitch, and French knot.

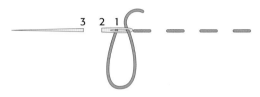

Running Stitch

Stem Stitch

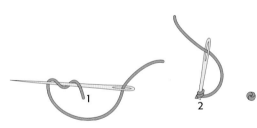

French Knot

Special Techniques

In this section, we'll discuss layering a quilt and machine quilting.

Machine Quilting

I love machine quilting because you can add as much quilting as you like without worrying that it will take too long. Machine quilting does not have to look like hand quilting. It offers you many ways to add interest and excitement to your quilt, and the results are beautiful. "Passionflower Pillow Cover" and "Norfolk Island Wreath Quilt" both feature machine quilting.

Layering and Pin Basting

Before you can quilt your project, you need to layer the backing, batting, and quilt top together. To begin, always use a backing and batting that are larger than the quilt top because the quilting process pulls the layers of the quilt in. You'll also find that it's easier to center the quilt top on larger pieces. If you're making a pillow cover, add 2" to the length and width of the top to determine the size of the backing and batting. For a queen-sized quilt, add 4". Any excess material will be trimmed away after quilting. Next, use masking tape to secure the pressed backing wrong side up to a hard surface such as a table or floor. Don't stretch the backing; just tape it so it is smooth. Then center the batting on top of the backing and smooth it out. Finally, center the quilt top on top of the batting and smooth it out from the center.

The biggest challenge you face when machine quilting is keeping the three layers of the project from shifting as you sew. Minor shifts create puckers; anything more can distort the entire surface of the quilt. The solution to the problem is correct pin basting.

Many machine-quilting instructions recommend that you use safety pins to baste the layers together, but there are disadvantages to that method. If you try to stitch close to the safety pins, the presser foot can get caught in them. If you remove the safety pins before stitching an area, the layers can shift. I recommend that you pin baste with ordinary straight pins—not the long ones made for quilts but the short, thin pins used for everyday sewing chores. (They are shorter than quilt pins but not as short as appliqué pins.) Shorter pins are easier to handle, and when you remove them, any stitches that have formed across their thin bodies snap back against the quilt instead of leaving permanent loops.

For small projects that do not have to be rolled or scrunched under the head of the machine, baste with the straight pins and simply sew over the pins as you work. For larger projects, first baste with safety pins spaced about 6" to 8" apart. Before machine quilting a specific row or area, replace the safety pins with the ordinary straight pins. Add as many pins as you need to keep the layers in place. Secure long seams for machine quilting by placing pins across the seam every 1½" or so. It takes a little longer to baste using this method, especially for large quilts, but it is definitely worth the effort.

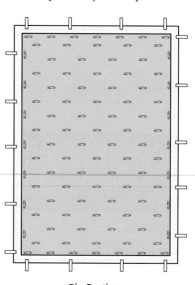

Pin Basting

Free-Motion Machine Quilting

The projects in this book are machine quilted with a free-motion technique called meandering. The resulting motifs look like pieces of a jigsaw puzzle. You attach a darning foot and drop the feed dogs on your sewing machine to quilt the free-motion lines. After you master this technique, you will find that learning other free-motion patterns is easy.

It is easier to visualize what happens when you sew with a darning foot and dropped feed dogs on your sewing machine if you understand what happens during typical sewing. A presser foot for basic sewing holds fabric snugly against the feed dogs at all times. When you choose a short stitch setting, the feed dogs grip the fabric and move it forward a short distance, which results in a short stitch. When you choose a long stitch setting, the feed dogs move the fabric a longer distance between stitches. If you take away either the feed dogs or the presser foot, the stitches won't form correctly because the two work together.

When you use a darning foot, it presses the fabric down when the needle is down and ensures that each stitch is formed correctly. However, when the needle goes up, the darning foot goes up too, so there's nothing to guide the fabric's movement, even if you choose a specific stitch length and leave the feed dogs engaged (up). When using a darning foot, the stitch length depends entirely on how fast you run the sewing machine and manually move the fabric.

Monofilament

Monofilament is a fine, transparent thread that is often used through the needle for machine quilting.

Monofilament produces quilting motifs that show up as raised areas on the quilt's surface, but the thread itself is camouflaged by the fabric. It is much more forgiving of errors than colored threads.

There are a few types of monofilaments that make better fishing line than quilting stitches! Choose a good-quality monofilament that's soft, fine, and pliable.

It is always a challenge to get the tension right when you use monofilament, especially with meandering, because the bobbin thread tends to come to the top when sewing curves. When that happens, the bobbin thread will be visible on the surface of the quilt. To avoid this problem, consider using monofilament in the bobbin as well as through the needle. I used monofilament in both places when I quilted the Passionflower block for the pillow cover on page 52. I followed a few guidelines when winding the bobbin, which made it work like magic. First, wind a layer of ordinary sewing thread onto the bobbin to cushion the monofilament. Then wind the monofilament slowly and evenly so that it doesn't stretch.

Rayon Thread

Rayon thread is fine, shiny, and lovely to use for machine quilting when you want a touch of color. It comes on big spools in many shades, including beautiful variegated versions.

Free-Motion Machine-Quilting Practice

1. Layer pieces of backing, batting, and a top fabric to make a practice sample that is at least 8" square.

2. Drop the sewing machine's feed dogs, choose a starting point, and bring the bobbin thread to the top to keep it from twisting underneath your sample. To pull the bobbin thread to the top, lower the darning foot and manually turn the machine's flywheel to lower the needle into the fabric. Keep turning until the needle comes back up through the layers. Raise the darning foot and gently tug on the top thread until the bobbin thread appears as a loop around it. On most machines, the right side of the loop is the thread tail. Pull it out of the fabric. The other

side goes into the bobbin, so tugging on it will simply empty the bobbin.

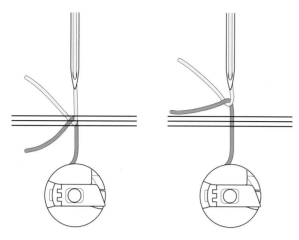

Pulling Bobbin Thread to the Top

3. Lower the darning foot. Then lower the needle manually into the same spot where the bobbin thread came up through the quilt. Start running the sewing machine's motor slowly and moving the sample slowly to make four to six very small stitches that will lock the threads. Increase the machine's speed to an even, medium rate and begin moving the sample in any direction to create smooth, random lines. Avoid sewing over previous stitches. Practice making the stitches shorter by moving the sample slowly and then move the sample faster to make longer stitches. Finish with four to six very small stitches and clip the threads close to the fabric.

Hetty's Hint

If you have ever driven a manual transmission car, you know that you can listen to the engine and tell instinctively when its speed is correct for changing gears. Your ears, eyes, hands, and feet must all work together. Free-motion machine quilting is a similar experience. You listen to your sewing-machine motor and keep it at an even speed with your foot while you use your hands to move the quilt evenly and smoothly. And you use your eyes to make sure that everything is working!

Machine-Quilting Tips

- To avoid machine tension problems, use the same thread in the bobbin as in the top.

- It is unnecessary for the quilting on the back of your project to blend with the backing fabric. Machine quilting that looks great on the front of the project will also look great on the back; there's no need to hide it!

- Move the quilt in any direction: up, down, right, left. If you keep the machine speed constant and move the quilt quickly, you'll have long stitches. If you move the quilt slowly, you will have short stitches.

- If your sewing-machine manual instructs you to cover the feed dogs with a little plate to disengage them, forget it! The plate will form a lump that can be distracting and leave less room for the thickness of the quilt. Drop the feed dogs if it is easy to do so. If not, setting the stitch length to zero will keep the feed dogs from moving.

- Keep your shoulders and neck relaxed. Remember to stop frequently to reposition your hands.

- Stopping with the needle in the quilt will hold the layers in place and help you avoid making a long stitch when you start again.

- Practice with a thread that contrasts with the quilt fabric so that you can see how well you are doing.

- The sooner you allow yourself to graduate to a real project, the sooner your skills will improve.

- Don't forget to breathe!

The section that follows explains how to make a shadow appliqué block. Please read the instructions carefully. You may need to refer back to this section for more detailed explanations while following the project instructions.

Layout Options

There are two methods you can use to position the appliqué pieces onto the background fabric, and neither involves tedious tracing of the designs. The most suitable option for a particular block or project is given with the project instructions.

Option 1: Fold the background as directed in the block directions to make horizontal, vertical, and diagonal creased lines that will serve as layout guidelines for appliqué pieces. The creases correspond with the dashed lines on each block diagram.

Option 1 is the easiest method. It is suitable for blocks with flowers and leaves that have simple shapes and are easy to arrange on the layout guidelines. If necessary, measure the distance from the center of the flower or leaf to the center of the block for consistent and accurate positioning. This option is used for the Iris, Vinca, Daisy, Camellia, and Morning Glory blocks.

Option 2: Crease the background to create guidelines as you did for option 1. Make a full-size pattern of the block diagram to place underneath the background by enlarging the block diagram 500% so that it measures 16". The lines will be visible through most light-colored background fabrics, enabling you to position appliqué pieces exactly. Use option 2 when flowers and leaves are made up of a combination of several appliqué pieces that must be positioned accurately. The Bougainvillea, Strelitzia, Hibiscus, Carnation, Passionflower, Nasturtium, and Daffodil blocks all require the use of option 2.

Note that there is an exception to the "no tracing" rule stated at the beginning of this section, and it occurs when you use option 2 with dark background fabrics. If the pattern is not visible when it is placed under the background, you will need to trace the pattern onto the fabric. Tape the pattern, face up, to a light box. Then tape the background fabric, centered and right side up, on top of the pattern. Trace the pattern onto the fabric with a light-colored pencil. If you do not have a light box, tape the pattern and background to a window or to a glass table with a light placed beneath it. Trace the pattern.

Getting Started

1. If indicated, enlarge the block diagram by 500% so that it measures 16" square. Choose your background and appliqué fabrics, and select the organza color. Place the appliqué fabrics on the background fabric, cover them with organza, and check the effect. If the combination looks good, continue to step 2. If it does not, try different combinations of fabrics and organza until you are happy with the results.

2. Tear a 19" x 19" piece of organza. Cut a 16½" x 16½" background piece, which includes a ¼" seam allowance.

3. To make appliqué placement guidelines, fold the background in half and press the fold lightly. Fold the background in quarters and press; then fold diagonally and press again. Press firmly enough to leave guidelines but not so heavily that the creases remain indefinitely. Unfold.

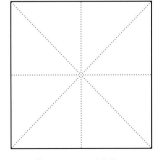

Placement Guidelines

Preparing Appliqué Pieces

1. Select an appliqué shape from the pattern section of your block instructions. Place fusible web over the shape, paper side up. Trace the shape with a permanent marker. Move the fusible web and continue tracing until you have the required number of that shape. All tracings should be close together. Mark the pattern letter on each traced shape.

Tracing Appliqué Shapes

2. Cut the shapes out as a group, leaving a small amount of fusible web around the group's outer margin.

3. Place the group, adhesive side down, on the wrong side of the appliqué fabric. Fuse it to the fabric with a dry iron. Cut the shapes out exactly on the marked lines. Each shape is now like an iron-on patch.

4. Repeat for all other shapes.

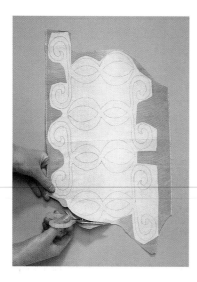

Cutting Out Appliqué Pieces

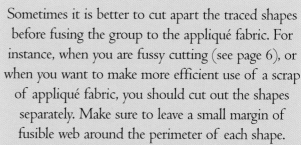

Hetty's Hint

Sometimes it is better to cut apart the traced shapes before fusing the group to the appliqué fabric. For instance, when you are fussy cutting (see page 6), or when you want to make more efficient use of a scrap of appliqué fabric, you should cut out the shapes separately. Make sure to leave a small margin of fusible web around the perimeter of each shape.

Shadow appliqué pieces are usually cut without a seam allowance and without underlaps (extra appliqué fabric covered by overlapping pieces). If an appliqué piece goes underneath another piece, it is indicated by a dotted line on the block diagram and noted in the instructions.

Fusing Pieces to the Background for Layout Option 1

1. Peel the paper off the appliqué pieces and place the pieces, adhesive side down, onto the right side of the background. The dashed lines on the block diagram represent the creased guidelines on the background. Wherever necessary, measurements from the center of the block to the center of the piece are also given in the block instructions.

2. Use an iron with steam to fuse the pieces in place. Refer to the instructions that came with the fusible web to determine the iron's heat setting.

Fusing Pieces to the Background for Layout Option 2

1. Make an ironing pad approximately 18" square if your ironing board is too narrow to accommodate the entire block. An old cotton blanket or a few layers of cotton batting, covered with an old sheet, makes an excellent ironing pad.

2. Place the enlarged pattern, right side up, on the ironing pad. Place the background on top, right side up. The pattern should be visible through the background.

3. Match the creased guidelines on the block background to the dashed lines on the pattern. The seam allowances of the background should extend ¼" beyond the block edges on the pattern.

4. Peel the paper off the first appliqué piece. Position the piece, adhesive side down, on the background. Use the point of the iron to fuse a small portion of the piece to the background—just enough to keep the piece from moving. Partial fusing prevents the pattern underneath from curling, which sometimes happens when the pattern gets too hot. Repeat until all pieces are partly fused.

5. Remove the pattern and finish fusing the appliqué pieces. Use an iron with steam. Refer to the instructions that came with the fusible web to determine the iron's heat setting.

Adding Organza

1. After all the appliqué pieces are fused to the background, check the surface of the block and remove any loose threads or fluff. Press the organza with a cool iron if necessary.

2. Center the oversized organza on the block. Using straight pins, pin it from the center out, about every 4". Baste the layers together securely with white or cream thread, stitching through the appliqué pieces. Baste in straight lines, vertically and horizontally, to form a grid. Keep the lines approximately 1½" apart and remove the pins as you baste. Do not take a shortcut when basting. If the block is not well basted, the background and organza layers will shift and distort when you stitch around the appliqué pieces. If that happens, it will be too late to fix the problem.

   Place the final row of basting stitches at the edge of the block, within the ¼" seam allowance. Keep it separate from the other basting rows because it will not be removed.

Organza

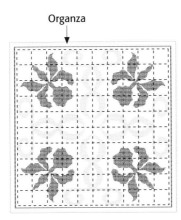

3. Place the block face down and press it lightly so that it is nice and flat.

Stitching around Appliqué Pieces

1. Choose embroidery floss that blends or contrasts with the appliqué piece. Cut two strands of floss, each approximately 18" long. Thread the strands onto an embroidery or crewel needle; an embroidery hoop is unnecessary.

2. Make a small knot at one end of the strands and pull the needle through from the back of the piece. Make small, even running stitches along the inside edge of the appliqué pieces; the stitches should be approximately ¹⁄₁₆" in from the edge. Stitch through the layers of organza, appliqué, and background. Then finish by weaving the floss through the stitches on the wrong side of the block. Sew another line of small, even running stitches along the outer edge of the piece, right against the appliqué edge, but this time the stitches should go through the organza and background only. Some of my students like to align these stitches with the previous running stitches, but it is unnecessary.

Adding Embroidery

Using a mechanical pencil, add guidelines for embroidery as indicated on the pattern. You'll only need to embroider stem stitches and French knots. Where fine lines are required, such as for leaf veins, use one strand of embroidery floss. Use two strands for heavier lines and French knots. I prefer to use a single strand for all stitching in smaller blocks.

Finishing the Block

1. Carefully remove all basting stitches except those at the very edges of the block. Work from the wrong side of the block to avoid snagging the organza with your stitch removal tool. Trim the excess organza, leaving a ¾" seam allowance.

2. Place the block face down on a towel and press it carefully with an iron on the steam setting. You may notice that the stitching has pulled the appliqué pieces in a little. If this is the case, gently pull the block into shape while pressing. Pull only in the direction of the grain of the background fabric; that is, from side to side or top to bottom. Pulling diagonally will distort the block.

3. Turn the block right side up. The purpose of the towel was to keep the appliqué work from being flattened, so it should puff out a little. The organza should be nearly invisible. The block is now ready to be used in a quilt or other project.

Iris Block Stitched with a Variety of Thread Colors

Cleaning Your Finished Projects

Polyester organza is quite strong. However, it does fray easily and sharp objects can damage it. If you follow the basting instructions on page 13 and leave a ¾" seam allowance as instructed in each pattern, fraying shouldn't be a problem. Wash by hand or use the gentle cycle on your washing machine. Use a detergent meant for delicate fabrics. If your finished project is quite large, it can be dry-cleaned, but discuss with your dry cleaner the need to treat the project delicately and to not press it after the cleaning process.

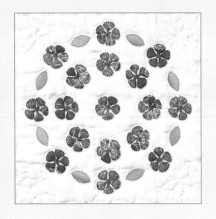

Iris Block

Finished block size: 16"

*This block was the first one I designed for this series.
It is the perfect block to start with because it is
very simple, with only eight appliqué pieces.*

Materials

Yardage is based on 42"-wide fabric unless otherwise noted.

- ¾ yard of cream organza for overlay
- ⅝ yard of cream tone-on-tone print for background
- 8" x 20" piece of purple print for flowers
- 8" x 30" piece of green print for leaves
- ¼ yard of fusible web
- Embroidery floss to match or contrast with appliqué fabrics
- Basic tools and supplies (see page 5)

Cutting

Refer to page 18 for appliqué patterns and "Preparing Appliqué Pieces" on page 12 for preparation and cutting instructions.

From the cream print, cut:

1 square, 16½" x 16½"

From the purple print, prepare and cut:

4 of pattern A

From the green print, prepare and cut:

4 of pattern B

From the cream organza, tear:

1 square, 19" x 19"

Note: Although each leaf (B) looks like it is made from two interlocking parts, it is cut from a single piece of fabric. Decorative stitching creates the over-and-under effect.

Making the Iris Block

Refer to "Making a Shadow Appliqué Block" on pages 11–14 for detailed instructions. Use layout option 1.

1. Crease guidelines in the background square.

2. Fuse the appliqué pieces to the background, using the creased guidelines and the block diagram for correct placement. The center of each iris is placed 6¼" from the center of the background.

3. Baste the organza over the block.

4. Mark lines on the leaves as shown. Stitch around the appliqué pieces and on the marked lines with a running stitch.

5. Trim the organza, leaving a ¾" seam allowance. Remove all the basting stitches except those within the seam allowance. Press.

Iris Block Diagram

Iris Patterns

A

B

Embroidery lines

Finished block size: 16"

*Also known as periwinkle, this hardy
little flower brightens up many gardens.*

Materials

Yardage is based on 42"-wide fabric unless otherwise noted.

- ⌒ ¾ yard of cream organza for overlay
- ⌒ ⅝ yard of cream tone-on-tone print for background
- ⌒ ⅛ yard of blue print for flowers
- ⌒ 4" x 8" piece of green print for leaves
- ⌒ ¼ yard of fusible web
- ⌒ Embroidery floss to match or contrast with appliqué pieces
- ⌒ Basic tools and supplies (see page 5)

Cutting

Refer to the appliqué patterns below and "Preparing Appliqué Pieces" on page 12 for preparation and cutting instructions.

From the cream print, cut:

1 square, 16½" x 16½"

From the blue print, prepare and cut:

17 of pattern A

From the green print, prepare and cut:

8 of pattern B

From the cream organza, tear:

1 square, 19" x 19"

Making the Vinca Block

Refer to "Making a Shadow Appliqué Block" on pages 11–14 for detailed instructions. Use layout option 1.

1. Crease guidelines in the background square.

2. Fuse appliqué pieces to the background using the creased guidelines and the block diagram for correct placement. The inside circle of flowers is 3½" from the center of the background; the outside circle is 6" from the center.

3. Baste the organza over the block.

4. Stitch around the appliqué pieces with a running stitch. Add French knots to the flower centers.

5. Trim the organza, leaving a ¾" seam allowance. Remove all the basting stitches except those within the seam allowance. Press.

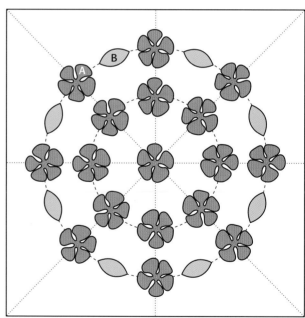

Vinca Block Diagram

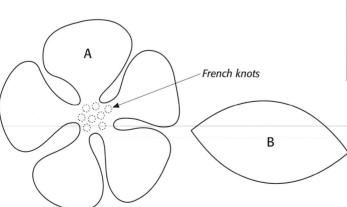

Vinca Patterns

Finished block size: 16"

There are many varieties of daisies, and no matter which color you choose, there is probably one just like it in nature. The inspiration for this block was the Hawksbury River daisy, with purple leaves and a golden yellow center.

Materials

Yardage is based on 42"-wide fabric unless otherwise noted.

- ¾ yard of cream organza for overlay
- ⅝ yard of cream tone-on-tone print for background
- 6" x 20" piece of purple print for flowers
- 5" x 14" piece of medium green print for leaves
- 3" x 6" piece of light green print for flower bases
- 3" x 3" piece of yellow print for flower centers
- ¼ yard of fusible web
- Embroidery floss to match or contrast with appliqué pieces
- Basic tools and supplies (see page 5)

Cutting

Refer to page 23 for appliqué patterns and "Preparing Appliqué Pieces" on page 12 for preparation and cutting instructions.

From the cream print, cut:

1 square, 16½" x 16½"

From the purple print, prepare and cut:

8 of pattern A

5 of pattern C

From the light green print, prepare and cut:

8 of pattern B

From the yellow print, prepare and cut:

5 of pattern D

From the medium green print, prepare and cut:

4 of pattern E

From the cream organza, tear:

1 square, 19" x 19"

Making the Daisy Block

Refer to "Making a Shadow Appliqué Block" on pages 11–14 for detailed instructions. Use layout option 1.

1. Crease guidelines in the background square.

2. Fuse the appliqué pieces to the background using the creased guidelines and the block diagram for correct placement. The B pieces overlap the A pieces; the D pieces are fused on top of the C pieces. One flower is in the center, and the centers of the other flowers are 5¾" from the center of the block. The leaves are placed 5" from the center of the block.

3. Baste the organza over the block.

4. Stitch around the appliqué pieces with a running stitch.

5. Trim the organza, leaving a ¾" seam allowance. Remove all the basting stitches except those within the seam allowance. Press.

Daisy Block Diagram

Daisy Patterns

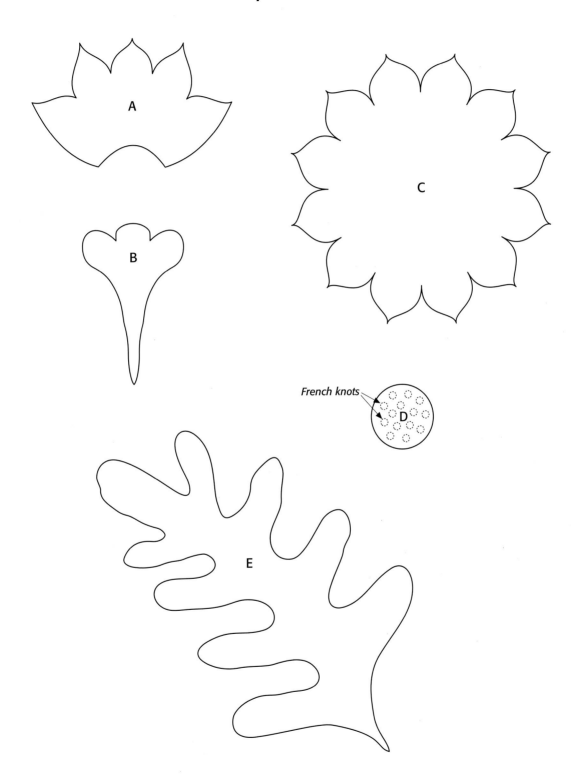

A

B

C

D

French knots

E

Camellia Block

Finished block size: 16"

Camellias may look delicate, but in the subtropical Australian climate where I live, they flower abundantly every winter without too much care or attention. Did you know that tea comes from the same plant family?

Three shades of magenta are used for the flowers in this block. Use shades that are quite close in value. For the sake of clarity, I've labeled them dark, medium, and light in the instructions.

Materials

Yardage is based on 42"-wide fabric unless otherwise noted.

- ¾ yard of cream organza for overlay
- ⅝ yard of cream tone-on-tone print for background
- 7" x 10" piece of dark green for leaves
- 7" x 7" square of dark magenta for flower petals
- 6" x 6" square of medium magenta for flower petals
- 4" x 4" square of light magenta for flower petals
- 3" x 3" square of yellow solid for flower centers
- ¼ yard of fusible web
- Embroidery floss to match or contrast with appliqué pieces
- Basic tools and supplies (see page 5)

Cutting

Refer to page 26 for appliqué patterns and "Preparing Appliqué Pieces" on page 12 for preparation and cutting instructions.

From the cream print, cut:

1 square, 16½" x 16½"

From the yellow, prepare and cut:

4 of pattern A

From the dark magenta, prepare and cut:

4 of pattern B

4 of pattern D

4 of pattern G

From the medium magenta, prepare and cut:

4 of pattern C

4 of pattern E

4 of pattern H

From the light magenta, prepare and cut:

4 of pattern F

From the dark green, prepare and cut:

4 of pattern I

8 of pattern Ir

From the cream organza, tear:

1 square, 19" x 19"

Note: Pieces B–H rotate clockwise on the tracing pattern, but they are fused onto the block in a counterclockwise manner. Since the shapes are similar, write the pattern letter on the paper side of the fusible web as you trace.

Making the Camellia Block

Refer to "Making a Shadow Appliqué Block" on pages 11–14 for detailed instructions. Use layout option 1.

1. Crease guidelines in the background square.

2. Fuse the appliqué pieces to the background using the creased guidelines and block diagram for correct placement. Start each flower by fusing its center (A) 5" from the center of the block.

3. Baste the organza over the block.

4. Stitch around the appliqué pieces with a running stitch. Embroider the leaf veins with a stem stitch and one strand of embroidery floss. The patterns below illustrate the embroidery used to embellish the flowers. Sew the stamens with long stitches and two strands of embroidery floss. Place a French knot at each stamen end. It isn't necessary to mark lines to follow for these stitches, because nature is never perfect either. Think of the stamens' radiating pattern as the numbers on a clock and follow this sequence: 12, 6, 9, and 3; then fill in the remaining lines freehand. Add extra French knots in the center of each flower.

5. Trim the organza, leaving a ¾" seam allowance. Remove all the basting stitches except those within the seam allowance. Press.

Camellia Block Diagram

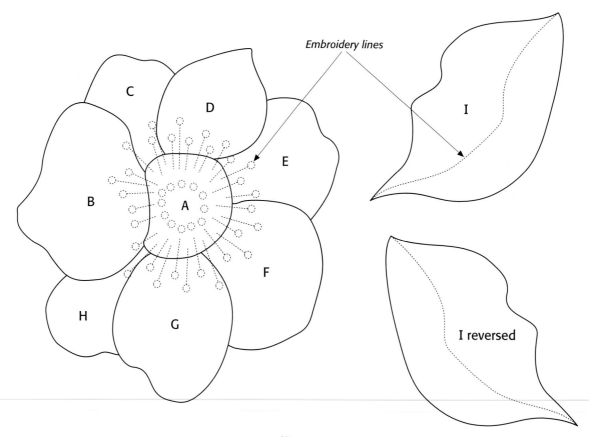

Embroidery lines

Camellia Patterns

Finished block size: 16"

*Morning glory—is it a flower? Is it a weed? It doesn't
matter what it is called. Its flowers are beautiful
and it will climb wherever it wants to!*

Materials

Yardage is based on 42"-wide fabric unless otherwise noted.

- ¾ yard of cream organza for overlay
- ⅝ yard of cream tone-on-tone print for background
- 6" x 8" piece of medium blue print for flowers
- 6" x 8" piece of dark green print for leaves and vines
- 6" x 7" piece of gold metallic organza for circular design elements
- 4" x 8" piece of light green print for leaves
- 4" x 4" square of apricot print for flower bases
- ¼ yard of fusible web
- Embroidery floss to match or contrast with appliqué pieces
- Basic tools and supplies (see page 5)

Cutting

Refer to page 29 for appliqué patterns and "Preparing Appliqué Pieces" on page 12 for preparation and cutting instructions.

From the cream print, cut:

1 square, 16½" x 16½"

From the gold organza, prepare and cut:

4 of pattern A

From the apricot print, prepare and cut:

4 of pattern B

From the medium blue print, prepare and cut:

4 of pattern C

From the dark green print, prepare and cut:

8 of pattern D

4 of pattern E

From the light green print, prepare and cut:

4 of pattern E

From the cream organza, tear:

1 square, 19" x 19"

Making the Morning Glory Block

Refer to "Making a Shadow Appliqué Block" on pages 11–14 for detailed instructions. Use layout option 1.

1. Crease guidelines in the background square.

2. Before fusing the appliqué pieces cut from the gold organza, test the fusing process with a small scrap to determine the correct temperature setting on your iron. Start with a low setting. Then fuse the appliqué pieces to the background using the creased guidelines and the block diagram for correct placement. Fuse the A pieces into a circle first, joining them where the B piece will be fused next. The C pieces overlap the B pieces. The dark green E pieces are fused around the block's center. The light green E pieces are fused around the design's outer perimeter.

3. Baste the organza over the block.

4. Stitch around the appliqué pieces with a running stitch. The flower petals (C) are made in one piece. Mark the flower petals and the leaf veins. Stitch with a stem stitch and a single strand of embroidery floss.

5. Trim the organza, leaving a ¾" seam allowance. Remove all the basting stitches except those within the seam allowance. Press.

Morning Glory Block Diagram

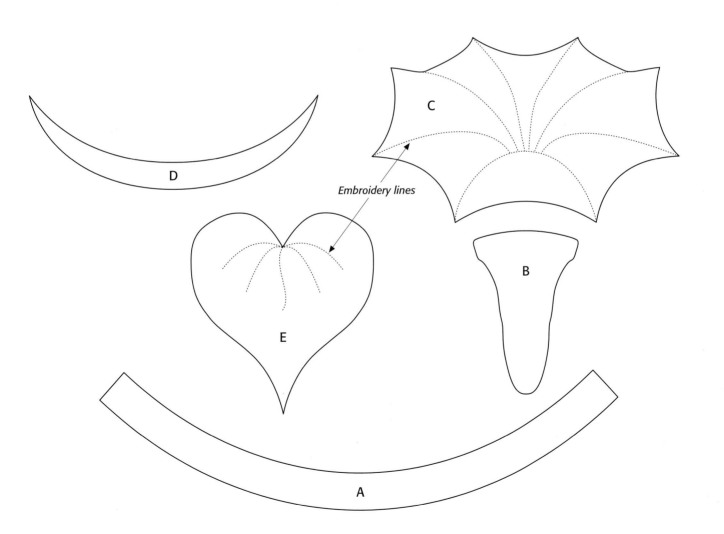

Embroidery lines

Morning Glory Patterns

Strelitzia Block

Finished block size: 16"

*The Strelitzia is a tropical flower
that is also called bird-of-paradise.*

I found a scrap of blue metallic fabric in my stash that was just right for the stamens, but any deep, bright blue will do. I used three shades of orange for the flowers in this block. The shades should be quite close in value, but for the sake of clarity I've labeled them light, medium, and dark in the instructions.

Materials

Yardage is based on 42"-wide fabric unless otherwise noted.

- ¾ yard of cream organza for overlay
- ⅝ yard of cream tone-on-tone print for background
- 8" x 8" square of light green print for leaves
- 7" x 7" square of dark green print for vines
- 4" x 6" piece *each* of light, medium, and dark orange prints for flowers
- 3" x 3" square of bright blue for stamens
- ¼ yard of fusible web
- Embroidery floss to match or contrast with appliqué pieces
- Basic tools and supplies (see page 5)

Cutting

Refer to page 32 for appliqué patterns and "Preparing Appliqué Pieces" on page 12 for preparation and cutting instructions.

From the cream print, cut:

1 square, 16½" x 16½"

From the dark green, prepare and cut:

4 of pattern A

From the dark orange, prepare and cut:

4 of pattern B

From the medium orange, prepare and cut:

4 of pattern C

From the light orange, prepare and cut:

4 of pattern D

From the bright blue, prepare and cut:

4 of pattern E

From the light green, prepare and cut:

4 of pattern F

From the cream organza, tear:

1 square, 19" x 19"

Note: Since shapes B, C, and D are similar, write the pattern letter on the paper side of the fusible web as you trace.

Making the Strelitzia Block

Refer to "Making a Shadow Appliqué Block" on pages 11–14 for detailed instructions. Use layout option 2.

1. To make a pattern for the block, enlarge the block diagram 500% so that it measures 16" square.

2. Crease guidelines in the background square.

3. With the enlarged pattern placed underneath the background, arrange the appliqué pieces and fuse them to the background. The D pieces should overlap the wide ends of the A pieces.

4. Baste the organza over the block.

5. Stitch around the appliqué pieces with a running stitch.

6. Trim the organza, leaving a ¾" seam allowance. Remove all the basting stitches except those within the seam allowance. Press.

Strelitzia Block Diagram
Enlarge 500%.

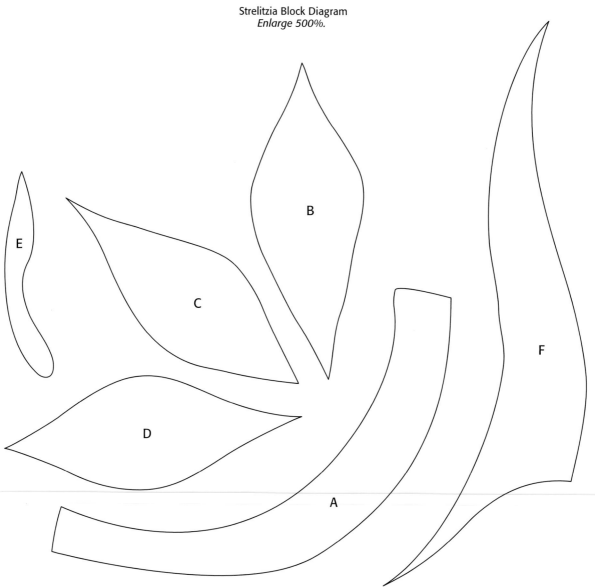

Strelitzia Patterns

Finished block size: 16"

This exuberant Peruvian native grows in many parts of the world. I love its bright and showy orange and yellow flowers.

Three shades of orange are used for the flowers. The fabrics I used are quite close in value, but for the sake of clarity I labeled them light, medium, and dark in the instructions.

Materials

Yardage is based on 42″-wide fabric unless otherwise noted.

- ¾ yard of cream organza for overlay
- ⅝ yard of cream tone-on-tone print for background
- 8″ x 16″ piece of light green print for leaves
- 6″ x 10″ piece of light orange print for flowers
- 6″ x 8″ piece of medium orange print for flowers
- 6″ x 6″ square of apricot print for flowers
- 4″ x 4″ square of dark orange print for flowers
- ¼ yard of fusible web
- Embroidery floss to match or contrast with appliqué pieces
- Basic tools and supplies (see page 5)

Cutting

Refer to page 35 for appliqué patterns and "Preparing Appliqué Pieces" on page 12 for preparation and cutting instructions.

From the cream print, cut:

1 square, 16½″ x 16½″

From the apricot print, prepare and cut:

4 of pattern A

From the light orange, prepare and cut:

4 of pattern B

4 of pattern D

From the medium orange, prepare and cut:

4 of pattern C

4 of pattern E

From the dark orange, prepare and cut:

4 of pattern F

From the light green, prepare and cut:

8 of pattern G

From the cream organza, tear:

1 square, 19″ x 19″

Note: The B–F petal pieces rotate clockwise on the tracing pattern, but they are fused onto the block in a counterclockwise fashion. Since the shapes are similar, write the pattern letter on the paper side of the fusible web as you trace.

Making the Nasturtium Block

Refer to "Making a Shadow Appliqué Block" on pages 11–14 for detailed instructions. Use layout option 2.

1. To make a pattern for the block, enlarge the block diagram 500% so that it measures 16″ square.

2. Crease guidelines in the background square.

3. Place the enlarged pattern underneath the background. Arrange the appliqué pieces and fuse them in place.

4. Center the organza on the pattern. Using a mechanical pencil, lightly mark the design that will be embroidered between the center A pieces. Baste the organza to the block, making sure that the center markings are aligned correctly with the fused appliqué pieces.

5. Stitch around the appliqué pieces with a running stitch. Use two strands of embroidery floss and a stem stitch to sew the design between the center A pieces. Using a mechanical pencil, lightly mark the leaf veins on the organza above the leaves. Use the pattern below as a guide, but remember that no two leaves are exactly the same—freehand vein lines will appear more natural.

6. Use a stem stitch and one strand of embroidery floss to stitch the leaf veins.

7. Trim the organza, leaving a ¾" seam allowance. Remove all the basting stitches except those within the seam allowance. Press.

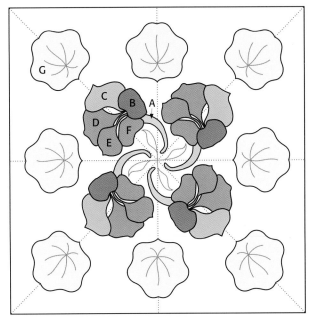

Nasturtium Block Diagram
Enlarge 500%.

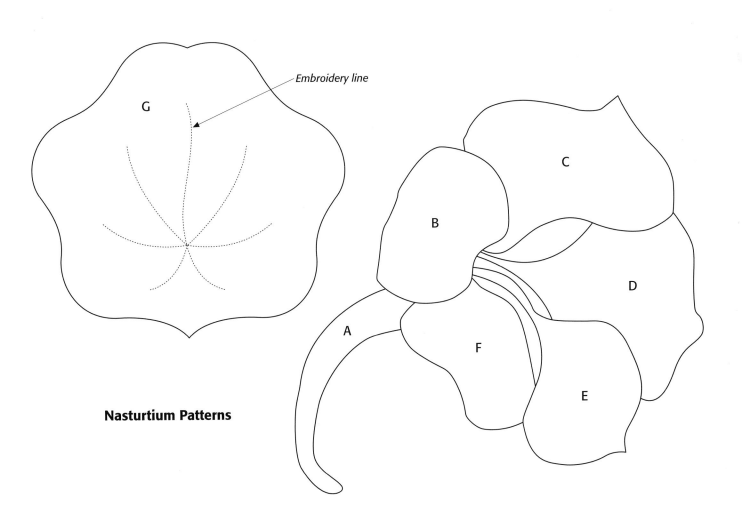

Embroidery line

Nasturtium Patterns

Finished block size: 16"

In tropical climates, this shrub flowers year-round. You'll see it in vibrant shades of purple, lavender, red, orange, or pink. The true flowers are quite small and insignificant inside the colorful bracts.

Materials

Yardage is based on 42"-wide fabric unless otherwise noted.

- ¾ yard of cream organza for overlay
- ⅝ yard of cream tone-on-tone print for background
- 8" x 8" square of dark green print for leaves
- 7" x 7" square of magenta solid for flower bracts
- 7" x 7" square of medium green print for leaves
- 6" x 6" square of red solid for flower bracts
- 7" x 4" piece of gold metallic organza for circular design
- 4" x 4" square of dark pink solid for flower bracts
- ¼ yard of fusible web
- Embroidery floss to match or contrast with appliqué pieces
- Basic tools and supplies (see page 5)

Cutting

Refer to page 38 for appliqué patterns and "Preparing Appliqué Pieces" on page 12 for preparation and cutting instructions.

From the cream print, cut:

1 square, 16½" x 16½"

From the gold organza, prepare and cut:

4 of pattern A

From the dark green print, prepare and cut:

4 of pattern B

4 of pattern G

4 of pattern I

From the magenta, prepare and cut:

4 of pattern C

From the red, prepare and cut:

4 of pattern D

From the dark pink, prepare and cut:

4 of pattern E

From the medium green print, prepare and cut:

4 of pattern F

4 of pattern H

From the cream organza, tear:

1 square, 19" x 19"

Making the Bougainvillea Block

Refer to "Making a Shadow Appliqué Block" on pages 11–14 for detailed instructions. Use layout option 2.

1. To make a pattern for the block, enlarge the block diagram 500% so that it measures 16" square.

2. Crease guidelines in the background square.

3. Place the enlarged pattern underneath the background. Before fusing the pieces cut from the gold organza, test the fusing process on a small scrap to determine the correct temperature setting on the iron. Start with a low setting. Then arrange the appliqué pieces and fuse them in place.

4. Baste the organza over the block.

5. Stitch around the appliqué pieces with a running stitch.

6. Trim the organza, leaving a ¾" seam allowance. Remove all the basting stitches except those within the seam allowance. Press.

Bougainvillea Block Diagram
Enlarge 500%.

Bougainvillea Patterns

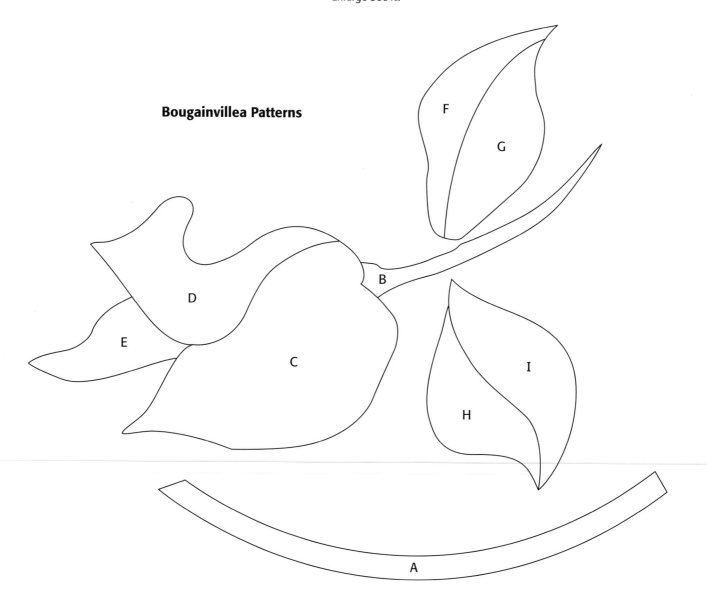

Finished block size: 16"

Hibiscus flowers can be found in many different colors and sizes. The hibiscus that this block was patterned after is a particular favorite of my husband's and mine. We take cuttings whenever we move so that we always have one in the garden. The pink flowers look delicate but the shrub does not require much attention, apart from a bit of water in dry weather and a good pruning once in a while.

If a flower has several petals, using the same fabric for all of the petals can make the flower look flat and uninteresting. For the Nasturtium and Camellia blocks, I achieved more depth by choosing fabrics in several shades of the same color. For the Hibiscus block, I used a marbled fabric with various pinks that formed a subtle tone-on-tone stripe for a realistic effect. I cut each petal with the stripe running from the center of the flower to the outside of the petal. To help you cut your pieces, the stripe direction is indicated on each petal pattern by an arrow.

Materials

Yardage is based on 42"-wide fabric unless otherwise noted.

- ¾ yard of cream organza for overlay
- ⅝ yard of cream tone-on-tone print for background
- ⅛ yard of pink tone-on-tone striped print for flowers
- 8" x 8" square of dark green print for leaves
- ¼ yard of fusible web
- Embroidery floss to match or contrast with appliqué pieces
- Basic tools and supplies (see page 5)

Cutting

Refer to page 41 for appliqué patterns and "Preparing Appliqué Pieces" on page 12 for preparation and cutting instructions.

From the cream print, cut:

1 square, 16½" x 16½"

From the pink print, prepare and cut:

4 of pattern A

4 of pattern B

4 of pattern C

4 of pattern D

4 of pattern E

From the dark green, prepare and cut:

8 of pattern F

From the cream organza, tear:

1 square, 19" x 19"

Note: The arrow on each pattern indicates the direction of the fabric stripe. Pieces A–E rotate clockwise on the tracing pattern, but they are fused to the block in a counterclockwise fashion. Since the shapes are similar, write the pattern letter on the paper side of the fusible web as you trace.

Making the Hibiscus Block

Refer to "Making a Shadow Appliqué Block" on pages 11–14 for detailed instructions. Use layout option 2.

1. To make a pattern for the block, enlarge the block diagram 500% so that it measures 16" square.

2. Crease guidelines in the background square.

3. Place the enlarged pattern underneath the background. Arrange the appliqué pieces and fuse them in place.

4. Baste the organza over the block.

5. Stitch around the appliqué pieces with a running stitch. Using the patterns on page 41 as a guide, mark leaf veins and flower stamens. Stitch veins with a stem stitch and a single strand of embroidery floss. Stitch stamens with a stem stitch and two strands of embroidery floss. Add French knots with two strands of embroidery floss.

6. Trim the organza, leaving a ¾" seam allowance. Remove all the basting stitches except those within the seam allowance. Press.

Hibiscus Block Diagram
Enlarge 500%.

Hibiscus Patterns

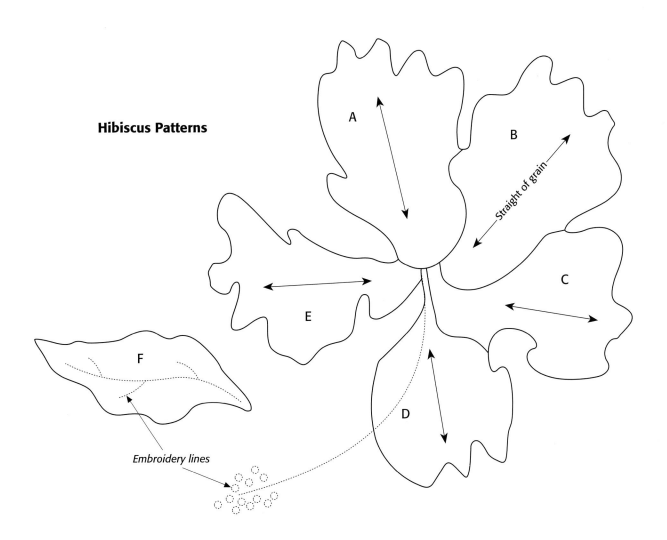

Straight of grain

Embroidery lines

Carnation Block

Finished block size: 16"

*Carnations are one of the most popular
cut flowers. We give and receive them to
celebrate, congratulate, and comfort.*

Use three different reds for the flowers. They can be close in value or the same color cut from different prints. For the sake of clarity, I've labeled the prints light, medium, and dark in the instructions.

Materials

Yardage is based on 42"-wide fabric unless otherwise noted.

- ¾ yard of cream organza for overlay
- ⅝ yard of cream tone-on-tone print for background
- 10" x 10" square of light red print for outer flower petals
- 7" x 7" square of medium red print for inner flower petals
- 5" x 5" square of dark red print for flower centers
- 4" x 4" square of fine red-and-white stripe for flower buds
- ⅛ yard of light green print for leaves
- ¼ yard of fusible web
- Embroidery floss to match or contrast with appliqué pieces
- Basic tools and supplies (see page 5)

Cutting

Refer to page 44 for appliqué patterns and "Preparing Appliqué Pieces" on page 12 for preparation and cutting instructions.

From the cream print, cut:

1 square, 16½" x 16½"

From the light red print, prepare and cut:

4 of pattern A (Cut out shaded area to reduce bulk.)

From the medium red print, prepare and cut:

4 of pattern B

From the dark red print, prepare and cut:

4 of pattern C

From the light green, prepare and cut:

4 of pattern D

4 of pattern F

4 of pattern G

4 of pattern H

4 of pattern Hr

From the red-and-white stripe, prepare and cut:

4 of pattern E (Refer to the arrow on the pattern for stripe direction.)

From the cream organza, tear:

1 square, 19" x 19"

Making the Carnation Block

Refer to "Making a Shadow Appliqué Block" on pages 11–14 for detailed instructions. Use layout option 2.

1. To make a pattern for the block, enlarge the block diagram 500% so that it measures 16" square.

2. Crease guidelines in the background square.

3. Place the enlarged pattern underneath the background. Arrange the appliqué pieces and fuse them in place. Note that piece B overlaps piece A, and piece C overlaps piece B.

4. Center the organza on the pattern. Using a mechanical pencil, lightly mark the stems and spiral design at the block's center. Baste the organza over the block, making sure that the stems and spiral design are aligned correctly with the fused appliqué pieces.

5. Stitch around the appliqué pieces with a running stitch. Then embroider the stems and spiral design with two strands of embroidery floss and a stem stitch.

6. Trim the organza, leaving a ¾" seam allowance. Remove all the basting stitches except those within the seam allowance. Press.

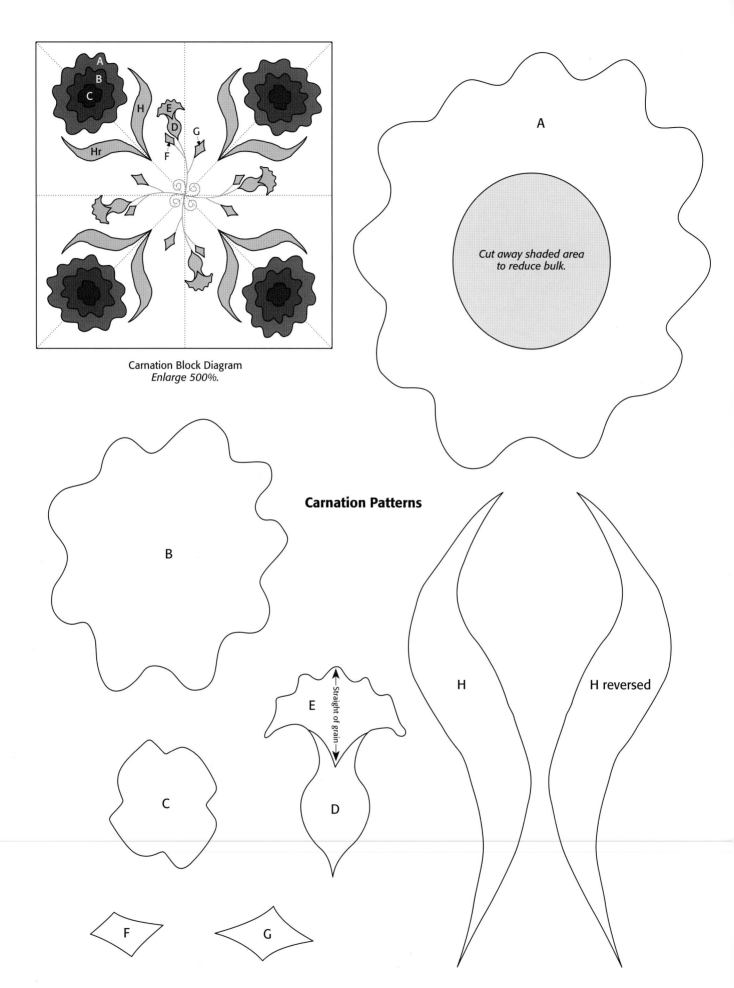

Carnation Block Diagram
Enlarge 500%.

A

Cut away shaded area
to reduce bulk.

Carnation Patterns

B

←Straight of grain→

E

C

D

H   H reversed

F   G

Passionflower Block

Finished block size: 16"

You might be interested to know that there are two types of passionflowers: one with edible fruit and one that is ornamental. The passionflower's edible fruit comes from a purple flower, similar to the one shown here, and the ornamental variety has huge, brilliantly colored red blooms.

When I studied the passionflower, I was intrigued by the way its fringed corona looks like threads radiating from a center. I was excited to find that I could replicate that look in shadow appliqué! Make sure you use a print fabric for the flower, preferably one with a linear design; it will become a circle in the finished flower.

Materials

Yardage is based on 42"-wide fabric unless otherwise noted.

- ¾ yard of cream organza for overlay
- ⅝ yard of cream tone-one-tone print for background
- ⅛ yard of dark green print for leaves
- 1½" x 40" piece of blue-and-purple stripe, with stripe running lengthwise, for flowers
- 5" x 5" square of dark purple print for passion fruits
- 4" x 4" square of light green print for flower bases
- 3" x 3" square of medium purple for flower buds
- ¼ yard of fusible web
- Parchment paper or appliqué pressing mat
- Embroidery floss to match or contrast with appliqué pieces
- Basic tools and supplies (see page 5)

Cutting

Refer to page 48 for appliqué patterns and "Preparing Appliqué Pieces" on page 12 for preparation and cutting instructions.

From the cream print, cut:

1 square, 16½" x 16½"

From the medium purple print, prepare and cut:

4 of pattern A

From the light green print, prepare and cut:

4 of pattern B

From the dark purple print, prepare and cut:

4 of pattern C

From the dark green print, prepare and cut:

4 of pattern D

4 of pattern Dr

From the piece of blue-and-purple stripe, cut:

4 strips, 1½" x 8½"

From the cream organza, tear:

1 square, 19" x 19"

Making the Flowers

1. Pull out the long threads on one side of a blue-and-purple strip until approximately ½" of fabric is left. Approximately 1" will be frayed.

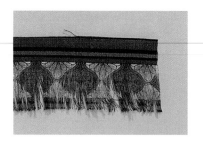

2. Hand sew small running stitches at the edge of the long side that has not been frayed. Use doubled thread in a matching color.

Gather fabric to make a circle.

3. Gather the fabric together as tightly as possible by sliding it along the gathering thread, leaving a long tail of thread on each end of the fabric strip. On the wrong side of the fabric, tie those ends together. If done tightly enough, the right and left ends of the fabric strip will meet, forming a circle. Knot the threads securely. Trim threads close to the knot.

4. Cut a piece of fusible web slightly larger than the fabric circle. Place the circle, wrong side down, on the glue side of the fusible web. Brush out the frayed-edge threads so that they fan evenly from the center. An eyebrow brush or toothbrush will help.

Passionflower Fused to Fusible Web

5. Cover the fabric circle and fusible web with parchment paper or an appliqué pressing mat. Fuse.

6. Trim the excess fusible web even with the edge of the fabric circle.

Making the Passionflower Block

Refer to "Making a Shadow Appliqué Block" on pages 11–14 for detailed instructions. Use layout option 2.

1. To make a pattern for the block, enlarge the block diagram 500% so that it measures 16" square.

2. Crease guidelines in the background square.

3. Place the enlarged pattern underneath the background. Arrange the appliqué pieces and fuse them in place. The B pieces overlap the A pieces.

4. Baste the organza over the block.

5. Stitch around the appliqué pieces with a running stitch. Mark embroidery lines freehand, using the diagram below and the patterns on page 48 as guides. Use one strand of embroidery floss to sew a stem stitch for veins and tendrils. Use two strands of embroidery floss for the French knots and the center design.

6. Trim the organza, leaving a ¾" seam allowance. Remove all the basting stitches except those within the seam allowance. Press.

Passionflower Block Diagram
Enlarge 500%.

Passionflower Patterns

A

B

C

D

Embroidery lines

D reversed

Finished block size: 16"

This outstanding design, with long leaves that are woven at the block's center, is worth the effort it takes to assemble it.

Note: To make appliqué placement easier, the pattern has been altered slightly from the one in the photo.

Materials

Yardage is based on 42"-wide fabric unless otherwise noted.

- ¾ yard of cream organza for overlay
- ⅝ yard of cream tone-on-tone print for background
- ⅜ yard of blue-and-green variegated print for leaves
- 7" x 7" square of medium yellow print for flowers
- 4" x 4" square of deep yellow-and-orange print for flower trumpets
- 3" x 3" square of pale yellow print for flower bases
- ¼ yard of fusible web
- Embroidery floss to match or contrast
- Basic tools and supplies (see page 5)

Cutting

Refer to page 51 for appliqué patterns and "Preparing Appliqué Pieces" on page 12 for preparation and cutting instructions.

From the cream print, cut:

1 square, 16½" x 16½"

From the medium yellow print, prepare and cut:

4 of pattern A

From the pale yellow print, prepare and cut:

4 of pattern B

From the deep yellow-and-orange print, prepare and cut:

4 of pattern C

From the blue-and-green variegated print, prepare and cut:

4 of pattern D

From the cream organza, tear:

1 square, 19" x 19"

Making the Daffodil Block

Refer to "Making a Shadow Appliqué Block" on pages 11–14 for detailed instructions. Use layout option 2.

1. To make a pattern for the block, enlarge the block diagram 500% so that it measures 16" square.

2. Crease guidelines in the background square.

3. Place the enlarged pattern underneath the background.

4. Peel the paper backing off the pieces and arrange them on the background, weaving the ends of the D pieces to create the center design. Handle the long pieces carefully. Use straight pins to anchor the leaves in place.

5. Fuse the pieces to the background when all the leaves are correctly placed. Fuse the flowers, with C pieces overlapping B pieces.

6. Baste the organza over the block.

7. Stitch around the appliqué pieces with a running stitch.

8. Trim the organza, leaving a ¾" seam allowance. Remove all the basting stitches except those within the seam allowance. Press.

Daffodil Block Diagram
Enlarge 500%.

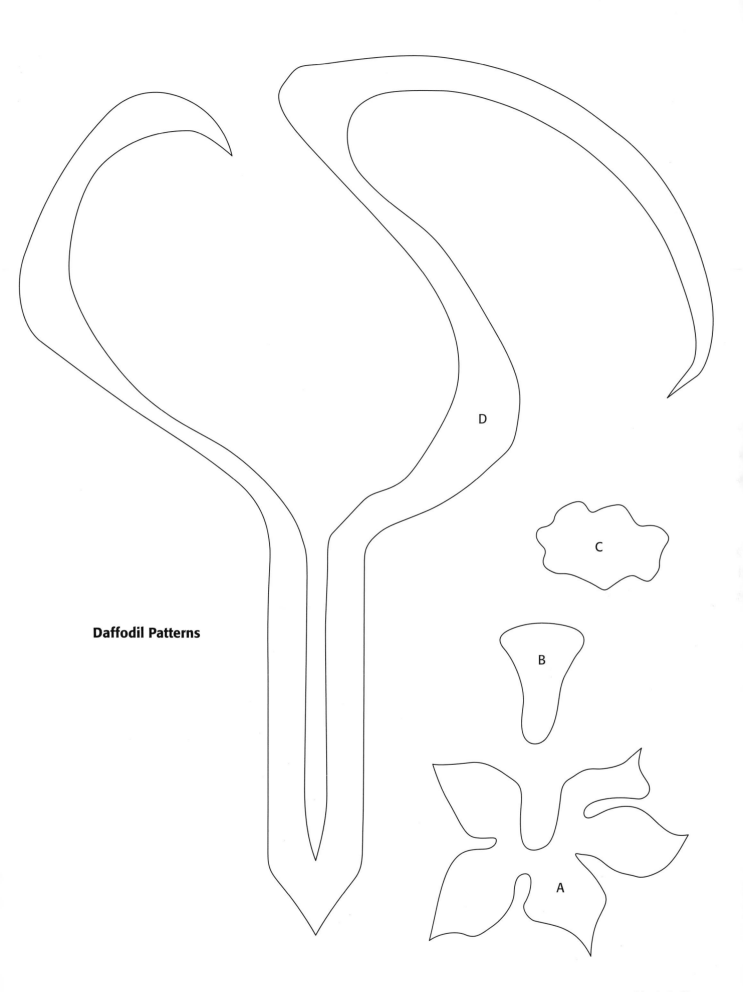

Daffodil Patterns

D

C

B

A

Passionflower Pillow Cover

Use these instructions to turn your Passionflower block into a gorgeous pillow cover. Of course, you can substitute this block with your own favorite from any of the block projects.

Materials

Yardage is based on 42"-wide fabric unless otherwise noted.

- 1 Passionflower block (see page 45)
- ⅝ yard of plum marble print for pillow back and ruffle
- ⅜ yard of green print for ruffle
- 18" x 18" square of any suitable fabric for block backing
- 18" x 18" square of thin batting
- Sewing thread to match plum marble print
- Monofilament for quilting
- Size 11 sewing-machine needles
- ¼" patchwork presser foot
- 3 plum-colored buttons, each 1¾" diameter
- 2 yards of strong thread, such as crochet cotton, in any suitable color
- Basic tools and supplies (see page 5)

Cutting

All cutting measurements include a ¼" seam allowance.

From the plum print, cut:

2 rectangles, 17" x 12"

3 strips, 3½" x 42"

From the green print, cut:

3 strips, 2½" x 42"

Quilting the Passionflower Block

I used clear monofilament to quilt the block. Refer to pages 8–10 for information on machine quilting.

1. Layer the block, the batting, and the backing.

2. Thread your sewing machine with monofilament through the needle and bobbin. Drop the feed dogs or set the stitch length to 0. Attach a darning foot. Put a size 11 needle in your machine.

3. Quilt on top of the running stitch that surrounds the outside edges of the appliqué pieces. Stitch over the tendrils, veins, and center design. Use free-motion meandering stitches in the open spaces.

4. Fold excess organza over the block and secure with pins to keep it out of the way. Trim backing and batting even with the edges of the block. Unpin the organza and trim to leave at least a ¾" seam allowance.

Making the Ruffle

1. Attach a patchwork presser foot to the sewing machine. Thread the top and bobbin of the machine with sewing thread.

2. Using straight seams, join the short ends of the three plum strips to make one long strip. Press the seams open to reduce bulk. Repeat for the three green strips.

3. Sew the green and plum strips together along one long side. Press the seam allowance toward the plum strip. With right sides together, sew the short ends of the unit together to form a circle. Press the seam open.

4. Press the unit in half lengthwise, wrong sides together and raw edges matched. One side of the strip will be plum; the other side will be green with a ½" band of plum along the folded edge. This green side is the right side of the ruffle. Divide the circle into four quarters, marking each quarter at the raw edges with a

pin. To help you divide the circle, think of it as the face of a clock and place a pin at 12, 3, 6, and 9.

5. Set the sewing machine to make a narrow zigzag stitch. Pin one end of the crochet thread within the seam allowance of the ruffle, anchoring the thread by wrapping it around a straight pin. Use a zigzag stitch to sew through both layers of the seam allowance, carefully maneuvering the crochet thread so that it is encased by the stitching but taking care to avoid sewing the thread to the ruffle.

Zigzag over Crochet Thread

Stitching the Ruffle to the Block

1. Remove the straight pin from the secured end of the crochet thread. Pull the thread out a bit so that it won't become lost in the seam allowance as you gather the ruffle. Pull on both ends of the crochet thread, gathering the ruffle evenly. Pin the ruffle to the block, right sides together. Match the center of each side of the block to each quarter-mark pin on the ruffle. Make sure to allow extra fullness at the corners or the ruffle may not lie flat. Pin across the seams at 1½" intervals. Tie the ends of the crochet thread together where they meet and trim the excess thread tails.

2. Use a scant ¼" seam allowance to carefully stitch the ruffle to the block.

Preparing the Pillow Back

1. Make a narrow hem along one 17" side of each of the two back rectangles. Fold the hem

to the wrong side of the backing, making a 3" facing. Press. On the left piece, make three buttonholes to fit your buttons. On the right piece, sew the buttons to correspond with the buttonholes.

2. Close the buttons to join the two pieces. Use a scant ¼" seam allowance to stitch the pieces together where they overlap on the outside edges. Trim to fit the block. Unbutton.

Stitch through all layers.

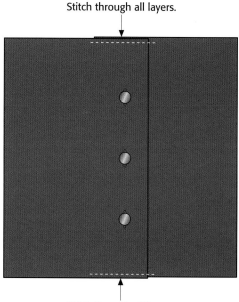

Stitch through all layers.

Sewing the Pillow Back to the Block

1. Position the pillow back, right side up, on a flat surface. Fold the block ruffle in toward the right side of the block. Then align the block, right side down, on top of the pillow back. Pin the units together carefully and frequently across the edges.

2. Stitch the back to the block with a full ¼" seam allowance so that the previous stitching will not show on the right side of the work. Keep one hand inside the pillow cover to prevent the gathers of the ruffle from getting caught in the stitching.

3. Turn the pillowcase right side out through the opening in the back of the pillow, pulling out the ruffle.

Finished quilt size: 31" x 31"

Historic Norfolk Island lies between New Zealand and Australia.
A penal settlement in colonial times, it is now a popular tourist
destination. This wall quilt features some of its native flora, the beautiful
pink Norfolk Island hibiscus and the stately Norfolk Island pine.

For the Norfolk Island hibiscus, I chose hand-dyed fabrics in five graduated shades of pink. They are quite close in value, but for the sake of clarity I have labeled them light, medium-light, medium, medium-dark, and dark in the instructions. The pine trees in the corners, which at first glance look like they are traditional pieced blocks, are assembled using shadow appliqué.

Refer to "Making a Shadow Appliqué Block" on pages 11–14 for detailed block instructions. For information about machine quilting, see pages 8–10.

Materials

Yardage is based on 42"-wide fabric unless otherwise noted.

- 1 yard of ivory organza for overlay
- ¾ yard of multicolored print for outer border (should match other colors in the quilt)
- ⅝ yard of white tone-on-tone for background center
- ½ yard of cloud print for background corner triangles
- 12" x 12" square *each* of 5 graduated shades of pink fabric for flowers
- ¼ yard of pink solid for inner border
- 10" x 20" piece of dark green print for pine tree branches
- 10" x 10" square of medium green for center leaf motif
- 5" x 10" piece of brown print for pine tree trunks
- 1¼ yards of fabric for backing and hanging sleeve
- ½ yard of chocolate brown solid for binding
- 34" x 42" piece of thin batting
- ½ yard of fusible web
- Thread in neutral color for machine piecing

- Clear monofilament and machine-embroidery rayon thread in pink for the top; thread to match or contrast with the backing fabric for the bobbin
- Size 11 sewing-machine needles
- Embroidery floss to match or contrast with appliqué fabrics
- ¼" patchwork foot
- Optional: open-toe appliqué foot or walking foot (see page 60)
- ½ yard of freezer paper
- Basic tools and supplies (see page 5)

Basic Cutting

All cutting measurements include a ¼" seam allowance where required.

From the cloud print, cut:

2 squares, 12⅞" x 12⅞"; cut each square in half once diagonally

From the white print, cut:

1 square, 17½" x 17½"

From the pink solid, cut:

4 strips, 1" x 42"

From the multicolored print, cut:

4 strips, 3½" x 42"

From the chocolate brown, cut:

4 strips, 2½" x 42"

From the backing and hanging-sleeve fabric, cut:

1 square, approximately 34" x 34"

1 strip, 6" x 30"

1 square, 8" x 8"

From the ivory organza, tear:

1 square, approximately 30" x 30"

From the thin batting, cut:

1 square, approximately 34" x 34"

1 square, 8" x 8"

Preparing and Cutting Appliqué Pieces

1. From the five shades of pink fabric, prepare and cut 40 flower appliqué pieces. Use the pattern on page 63. First trace a group of eight petals onto fusible web and fuse to the lightest shade of pink. Label the paper backing of each petal with the letter *L* (for lightest). Repeat for each shade, labeling each petal with the appropriate shade: *ML, M, MD,* or *D* for medium-light, medium, medium-dark, or dark.

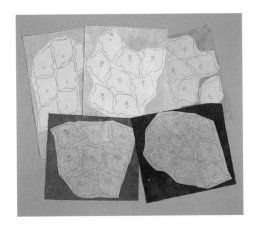

Petals Traced and Fused to Appliqué Fabric

2. Cut out each piece on the traced line, keeping the different shades separate.

3. From the dark green print, prepare and cut the pine tree triangles as follows. First trace two copies of the pine tree pattern on page 63 onto the paper side of fusible web. Each tracing will make two pine trees. Label each triangle as indicated on the pattern with the letter *A, B, Br,* or *C.*

4. Cut out each 6½"-square pine tree pattern, leaving a small allowance of fusible web around the perimeter of each. Fuse the squares to the wrong side of the dark green fabric. Cut out the triangles on the solid lines.

5. From the brown print, make the pine tree trunks as follows. First cut a piece of fusible web that measures 4" x 8". Fuse it to the wrong side of the fabric; then cut the fused piece into four strips, each ¾" x 7½".

6. From the medium green, prepare and cut eight leaf appliqué pieces. Use the pattern on page 63. First trace a group of eight leaves onto fusible web and fuse to the medium green fabric. Then cut out each piece on the traced line.

Fusing Appliqué Pieces to the Background

1. Fold the background triangles in half to find their centers. Crease each one to make layout guidelines.

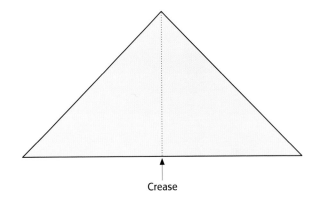

Crease

2. Fuse a pine tree trunk to a background triangle, centering it on the creased line. Position the bottom edge of the trunk piece even with the long edge of the background triangle. Pine tree triangles will overlap the trunk.

3. Arrange the pine tree triangles as shown in the diagram. Fuse the A triangles first; then follow with the B and Br triangles. Fuse the C triangles last.

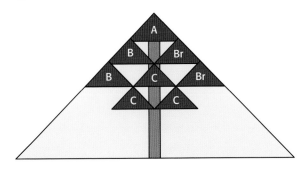

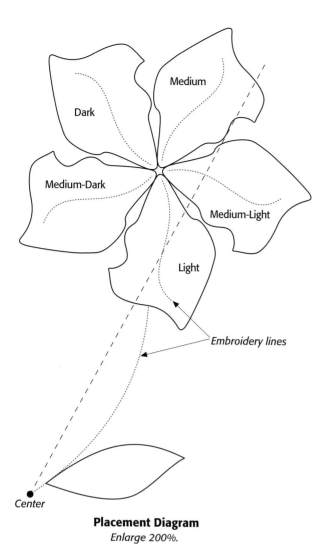

Placement Diagram
Enlarge 200%.

4. Stitch a background triangle to each corner of the white background square. Handle the bias edges of the triangles gently to avoid stretching the fabric. Press the seam allowances toward the background triangles.

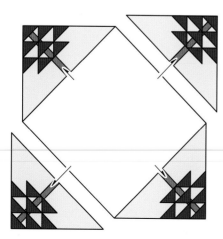

5. To make layout guidelines, fold the background square in half from top to bottom and crease lightly. Repeat from side to side, and then twice diagonally.

6. Using a photocopy machine, enlarge the placement diagram 200%.

7. Place the enlarged diagram underneath the background square; place one of the creased guidelines over the dashed line on the diagram. The center dot on the diagram should be exactly underneath the center of the background square.

8. Arrange and fuse one completed flower as shown in the diagram. Then position and fuse a leaf. Carefully rotate the background, placing another creased guideline over the diagram dashed line and keeping the centers of the diagram and background aligned. Fuse the next flower and leaf. Continue until all appliqué pieces have been fused to the background.

Adding Organza and Stitching

1. Baste the organza over the background.

2. Stitch around the pieces with a running stitch. Mark the veins and embroider them using a stem stitch and one strand of embroidery floss. Mark the stems and use two strands of floss to embroider them with a stem stitch.

3. Trim the organza, leaving a ¾" seam allowance. Remove all the basting stitches except those within the seam allowance. Press.

Making Mitered Borders

The following steps describe my favorite way to miter a border. If your project requires two or more borders, stitch the border fabrics together first and then miter the unit as if it were one fabric. Use a ¼" patchwork foot to sew ¼" seam allowances.

1. Stitch a narrow inner-border strip lengthwise to a wider outer-border strip. Repeat for the remaining three borders. Press seam allowances toward the darker fabric.

2. Fold each border in half crosswise and crease. Place a pin at the crease to mark the midpoint; then insert a pin exactly 12" from the midpoint on each side. Do not omit this step, because it forms an accurate frame to help keep your quilt square. With careful measuring, the borders will be nice and flat. Then fold each side of the quilt in half. Make a crease to mark the midpoint of the quilt edge on each side.

3. Pin the first border to one edge of the quilt, aligning the marked border center with the quilt-edge midpoint. The outer pins should be ¼" from the corners of the quilt. Stitch the border in place, starting and stopping at the outer pins. Backstitch at the beginning and end of the seam to lock the stitches. If necessary, ease or stretch the quilt edge to fit the border edge.

4. Repeat to add the other borders. Look at the wrong side of the quilt; the stitching lines should meet exactly. There should be no gaps

and seam lines should not go beyond each other at their ends.

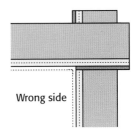

Wrong side

5. Turn the quilt right side up on an ironing board. Ensure that the quilt and the borders are straight and square. Fold the corner of one border under to make a 45° miter. The ends of both borders should be even. Use an iron to press the fold.

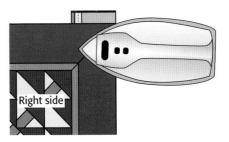

Right side

6. Fold the quilt diagonally. Stitch along the crease in the border, starting at the edge of the border and ending at the previous stitching line. Backstitch to lock the threads.

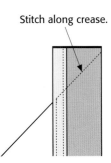

Stitch along crease.

7. With the right side of the quilt up, inspect the corner. The seam should run from the corner of the quilt to the corner of the border. The two sides of the border should form a square. You can check this by placing a quilter's ruler on the corner, aligning the corner of the ruler with the border corner. The edges of the border should be even with the edges of the ruler. If it looks correct, trim the seam allowance to ¼".

8. Repeat for all corners. Press the seams open.

Quilting the Top

"Norfolk Island Wreath Quilt" was machine quilt-ed. Use hand quilting if you prefer. The general instructions for machine quilting begin on page 8.

1. Create a practice quilting sample by layering 8" squares of backing, batting, and top fabric. Thread a size 11 needle with clear monofila-ment on top and your choice of color in the bobbin. The bobbin thread may blend or contrast with the backing fabric. Use the 8" sample square to test the stitch length and tension on your sewing machine.

2. When you are satisfied with your stitches, layer the quilt backing, batting, and top and secure them with straight pins.

3. Use a presser foot that will enable you to stitch approximately ⅛" outside the appliqué lines. Machine quilt around the pine trees.

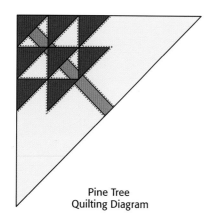

Pine Tree
Quilting Diagram

4. Switch to a darning foot. Drop the feed dogs or set the stitch length to 0. Machine quilt over the outside stitches that surround each petal, and up and down the veins. Outline the leaves in the same way.

5. Use a meandering stitch to fill in the open spaces, including the background triangles. Do not quilt the borders.

Quilting the Border

This is an easy technique that can be adapted to the borders on any quilt. It is not necessary to mark the borders.

1. Trace the border quilting pattern below eight times on freezer paper and cut it out.

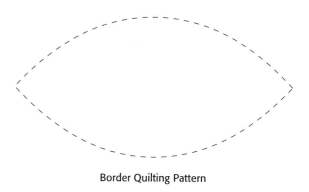

Border Quilting Pattern

2. Insert a straight pin along the diagonal seam line of the 3"-wide border, placing it 2⅛" from the inside corner of the border. Iron the freezer-paper shapes to the border, starting from the pin and working toward the center of each side. You'll iron four shapes point to point on one side of the pin and four on the other side. Remove the pin.

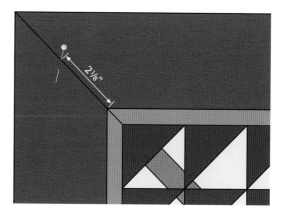

3. Thread your sewing machine with the pink rayon on top. Use the same color in the bobbin as you did for quilting the top. Pin baste every 1½" across the edges of the freezer paper to stop puckers. Set the stitch length at 3 and make sure the feed dogs are up. Use a normal sewing foot, an open-toe appliqué foot, or a

walking foot. I prefer to use an open-toe appliqué foot.

4. Start stitching at the point of the ellipse shape farthest from the diagonal seam, pulling the bobbin thread to the top to keep it from twisting underneath (see page 10). It is not necessary to lock the threads. Carefully sew along the edges of the freezer paper. Let the feed dogs move the quilt. If you don't push and pull on the quilt, it is unlikely that you will break the needle. Stitch the outside of the first ellipse and then the inside of the next, or vice versa. Continue stitching to the end.

Start stitching here.

5. Go back to the beginning and stitch the other side of the shapes.

6. Take the pins out and remove the freezer paper. Use the layered sample square to try out a decorative stitch. Test the stitch length, stitch width, and tension.

7. Stitch in the border again, covering the previous straight stitch with the decorative stitch. These stitches do not come out easily, so there is no need to backstitch. When you are finished, take all thread ends to the back of the quilt. Tie the ends together and use a needle to pull the ends between the layers of the quilt. Come up through the backing again and cut the ends of the threads.

8. Repeat on each corner, reusing the freezer-paper shapes if they are still good, or make new ones if they're not. This technique is easy and attractive, and it is fun to use one of your machine's decorative stitches.

Making the Mitered Binding and a Hanging Sleeve

You can make bindings with mitered corners several ways. The following is my favorite method. I've also included steps for adding a hanging sleeve.

1. Prepare the quilt for binding by trimming the backing and batting even with the top.

2. Carefully hand baste the three layers together in the seam allowance. Do this on a flat surface, pulling the basting thread so that the edge of the quilt lies flat on a table. Basting this way ensures that the binding does not need to be pinned and keeps the edge of the quilt from rippling when the binding is complete.

3. Use diagonal seams to join the binding strips into one long strip. Trim the seam allowances to ¼".

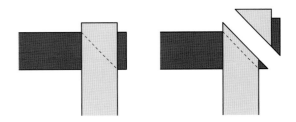

4. Press the seams open to reduce bulk. Press the strip in half lengthwise, wrong sides together. Trim the seam allowance nubs.

5. Fold the right sides of the hanging-sleeve strip together lengthwise. Stitch the short edges together. Turn the sleeve right side out and press.

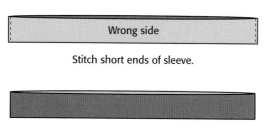

Stitch short ends of sleeve.

Turn right side out.

6. Center and pin the hanging sleeve to the back side of the quilt along the top edge, aligning the raw edge of the sleeve with the raw edge of the quilt. Pin an inch or so from the raw edge to keep the pins from getting stuck in the feed dogs when you sew, as this side will be on the bottom when you attach the binding.

7. Starting about halfway down one side of the quilt, align the binding along the front side of quilt. Match the raw edge of the binding with the raw edge of the quilt. Leave a few inches of binding free at the beginning. Start stitching; then backstitch to lock the stitches. Holding the binding in place, continue stitching the binding to the quilt and stop ¼" from the first corner. Backstitch to lock the stitches.

8. Remove the quilt from the machine. Fold the binding up, forming a diagonal fold. Then fold the binding back down, making the top fold of the binding level with the top of the quilt. Sew the binding to the next side, beginning at the top edge and stopping ¼" from the corner of the quilt as before.

Quilt front

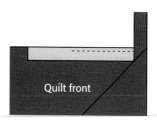

9. Continue around the quilt until the end of the binding meets the beginning. Backstitch to lock the stitches.

10. To join the ends, fold one end of the binding diagonally in one direction and the remaining end diagonally in the other direction. Hand stitch the ends together along the fold with small slip stitches. Trim to leave a ¼" seam allowance.

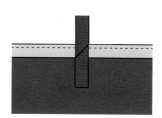

11. Turn the binding to the back of the quilt. The corners should fold into a perfect miter on the front, which needs no further stitching. Fold the binding snugly over the raw edges of the quilt so that there is no "empty" binding. Fold the corners into a miter. Stitch the edges and the miters with small, even slip stitches. The binding will be wider on the back than it is on the front.

12. Make a small pleat in the hanging sleeve across the top of the quilt. Hand-stitch the folded edge securely to the quilt backing. The extra fullness will ensure that the quilt will hang better on a rod.

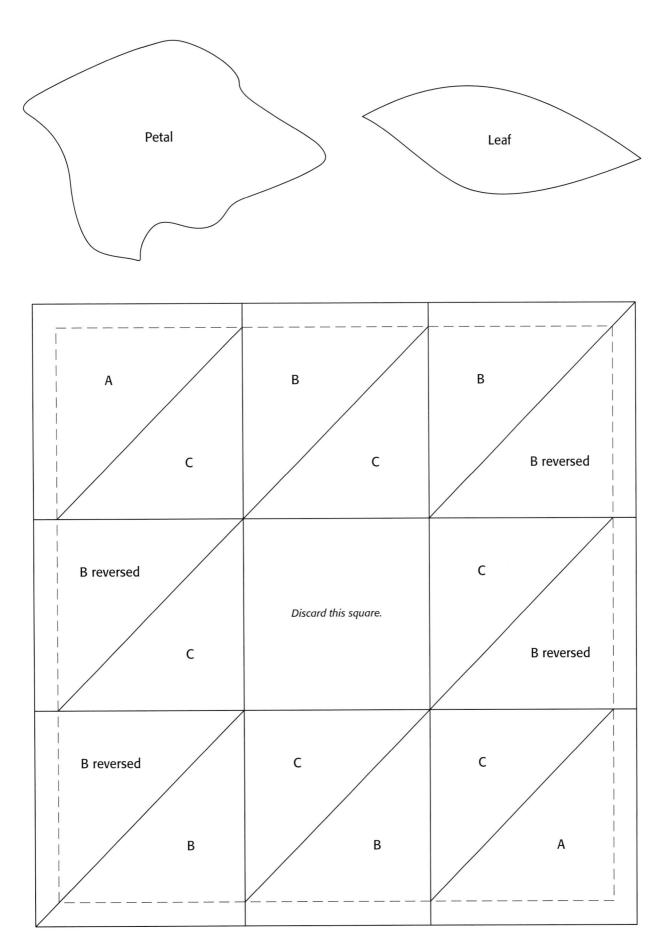

Petal

Leaf

A	B	B
C	C	B reversed
B reversed	*Discard this square.*	C
C		B reversed
B reversed	C	C
B	B	A

Pine Tree Pattern

About the Author

Born in the Netherlands, Hetty van Boven and her husband, Gerry, settled in Australia in 1965 soon after they married. Always interested in sewing, Hetty discovered patchwork and quilting in 1980 when she bought some American needlework magazines. Within a few years, she was teaching this exciting craft in her own area and writing for Australian patchwork and quilting magazines. Since the late eighties, Hetty has produced the "Double Wedding Ring Kit," an instruction book and set of heavy acrylic templates for rotary cutting. This kit is still in demand with quilters and teachers. In 1990 her book *From Australia, with Love* was published. In 1997, after teaching shadow appliqué for more than a decade, she self-published a set of shadow appliqué patterns titled "From my garden, with Love," which has now become *Shadow Appliqué.*

Hetty has taught shadow appliqué in Australia, the Netherlands, the United States, Canada, and on Norfolk Island. Her quilts have been displayed at major quilt exhibitions in Australia and the Netherlands. A special showing of Hetty's work was held at the Kenai Visitors and Cultural Center in Alaska for four weeks in 1999. Photographs of her work have appeared in publications in Australia, the Netherlands, the United States, and Canada.

Hetty and Gerry live in sunny Queensland, Australia. Hetty travels extensively to teach and share her passion for patchwork and quilting.